Terrance Talks Travel:
A Pocket Guide to
African Safaris

Terrance Zepke

Safari Publishing

All queries should be directed to:
www.safaripublishing.net

Library of Congress Cataloging-in-Publication Data

Zepke, Terrance

Terrance Talks Travel: A Pocket Guide to African Safaris

America/Terrance Zepke p. cm.

ISBN 978-0-9960650-2-3

Travel-Africa. 2. Adventure Travel Africa. 3. Safari-Africa. 4. Africa. 5. East Africa. 6. South Africa. 7. Africa-Tour Operators. 8. National Parks-Africa. Africa- Wildlife. 9. Family Safari-Africa. 10. Tanzania. 11. Kenya. 12. Botswana. 13. Nambia. 14. Zambia. 15. Zimbabwe. 16. Africa- Islands. 17. Africa- Game Reserves. 18. Africa-Kruger. 19. Africa-Masai Mara. I. Title.

First edition
10 9 8 7 6 5 4 3 2 1

CONTENTS

Introduction

I have been to Africa many times and still feel as if I've barely scratched the surface. There are so many things to do and see that it is a perfect vacation destination for all ages. In fact, one of the best family vacations you can have is a safari trip. Young and old can appreciate the many splendors and activities, such as a sunset cruise on the Zambezi River and seeing giraffes and gazelles up close during a bush walk. Africa holds a special place in my heart and I am sure that it will for you too—if you decide to participate in this truly once-in-a-lifetime experience.

But there's a lot you need to know before you go. For one thing, Africa is a continent—not a country. Fifty-four countries make up this enormous continent. In fact, Africa is the second largest continent in the world. Africa makes up more than twenty percent of our world's land mass. It is three times bigger than the United States of America.

Africa has more than 1 billion inhabitants from 3,000 ethnic groups. Each country has its own currency. Roughly 2,000 languages are spoken in Africa. South Africa alone has eleven official languages!

Some places in Africa are high in crime, just like other places around the world. Most of these are not even places where tourists go, such as The Democratic Republic of the Congo, Sudan, Somalia, and a few pockets of Nairobi and Zimbabwe. For the most part, however, Africa is quite safe.

While there are lots of other things to do in Africa besides safaris, let's face it, they are the main attraction—and rightfully so! For the most part, Africa's wildlife is confined to national parks and reserves. But then again, most of Africa is comprised of game reserves, World Heritage Sites, and national parks. There are hundreds, perhaps thousands, such places scattered throughout Africa. This book is about making sure travelers find the perfect safari experience *for them.* After all, a safari is not "one size fits all." One traveler may be looking for a particular experience, such as a birding safari in the Okavango Delta while another traveler is interested in gorilla trekking in Uganda. Some travelers will choose participatory camping safaris in Namibia while others prefer to stay in the luxurious William Holden Safari Club in East Africa. The point of this book is to make sure you know all the options and then take you step by step through the process of planning and booking your safari.

You may want to listen to my show on Blog Talk Radio, *Terrance Talks Travel: Über Adventures*, because Africa has been featured on several of these shows. The only thing I enjoy as much as traveling is writing and talking about it. I write a weekly *Terrance Talks Travel* blog, www.terrancetalkstravel.com, as well as post free travel reports, the latest travel news, and my 'Trip Pick of the Week'. I have appeared on many programs to share my expertise, such as the 'Good Morning Show', 'Travel with Rick Steves', and 'Around the World'. I have been featured in The *Washington Post, Publishers Weekly, AAA's Go Magazine, Boston Globe, San Francisco Chronicle, USA Travel Magazine, Detroit Free Press,* and *Associated Press.*

Safaris are among my favorite adventures, but since they are in sub-Saharan nations, travelers need to be prepared. After reading this reference, you'll learn everything you need to know. So keep reading and get ready for an adventure of a lifetime...

* * *

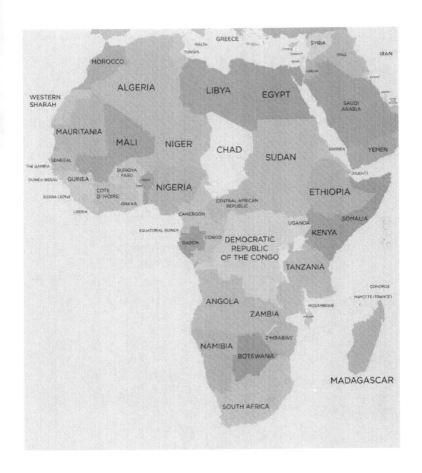

Map of Africa

Fun Facts

There are 54 countries in Africa and many offer safari options.

The newest country is South Sudan, which was established on July 9, 2011.

The most populated country is Nigeria.

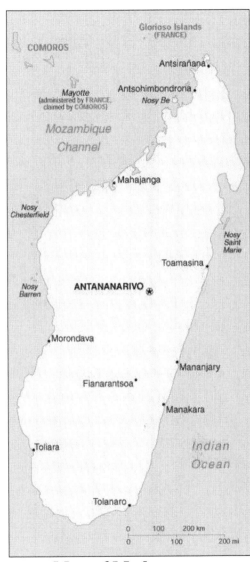

Map of Madagascar

Madagascar is the largest island in Africa and has been dubbed the "eighth continent of the world." This 350-mile wide by 1,000-mile long island has a diverse eco-system with many plants and animals that can't be found anywhere else in the world.

The largest waterfall in Africa is Victoria Falls, which is on the border of Zambia and Zimbabwe. It flows into the Zambezi River. Most visitors to the falls opt to take a sunset river cruise or to go whitewater rafting.

The longest river in Africa is the Nile, which also happens to the longest river in the world. It flows from northern Africa to Egypt.

Lake Victoria, which feeds into the Nile, is the largest lake in Africa and the second largest in the world.

The least populated country is The Seychelles, which is an archipelago of 115 islands in the Indian Ocean.

The Sahara is the biggest desert in Africa. It is close to 3.5 million miles.

The Equator is in Africa. It actually extends 2,500 miles through six countries: Congo, Democratic Republic of Congo, Gabon, Kenya, Somalia, and Uganda.

The tallest mountain in Africa is Mount Kilimanjaro in Tanzania.

Cairo (Egypt) is the most populated city with 17 million inhabitants.

Egypt is the most visited country. Millions of tourists come every year to see the Sphinx and the Pyramids. But South Africa may soon surpass it since it is such a close second.

Believe it or not, Sudan has more pyramids than Egypt. They are not as grand, but they total 223!

The least populated capital city is Maseru, which is the capital of the Kingdom of Lesotho. It has less than 15,000 residents.

The lowest point in Africa is Lake Assal, which is 515 feet below sea level!

The most visited countries in West Africa are Senegal and Gambia.

*   *   *

Ten Steps To Planning A Perfect Safari

If you're interested in going on a safari but you're not sure about where to go or how to proceed, these steps will show you the way. If you follow these ten steps, you will have assembled the perfect safari experience—for you! You should allow a minimum of six months to plan this properly. This will allow time to get vaccinations, visas, find cheap airfares, and most importantly, schedule travel during the best safari months. Even if you're planning on booking an all-inclusive safari package, you should know this information so that you can be sure which trip (and time of year) is the best option for you.

**Masai people live in Masai Mara
Kenya & Tanzania**

Step #1: Decide Where & How To Go

Africa is a continent with fifty-four countries.
Where you go depends on what you want to see
and do—and what your budget is. You can
choose from $100 a day overland safaris that
involve camping to $1,000 a day ultra-luxurious
private safari lodges with suites and spas. But
don't worry. There are lots of options in between
these two extremes. But first you need to figure
out what you want to see and do.

FYI: The "Big Five" refers to Leopards,
Lions, Rhinos, Elephants, and Cape Buffaloes.
The "Big Nine" also includes Hippos, Cheetahs,
Giraffes, and Zebras.

For most participants, the best safari experience will be in Southern Africa or East Africa. In terms of wildlife, both places offer roughly the same. There are larger numbers of some animals in East Africa's Masai Mara National Reserve and Serengeti National Park, such as zebras and wildebeests, while Southern Africa offers huge numbers of lions and elephants.

However, in terms of topography, they are very different. East Africa has miles of savannahs while Southern Africa has the Skeleton Coast (driest place in Africa), the Cape Peninsula (whale watching and shark cage diving), and the Okavango Delta (wetlands). East Africa has the famed Mount Kilimanjaro while Southern Africa offers Victoria Falls.

Another distinction is that participants enjoy game drives in pop-up jeeps in East Africa, meaning the roof pops up so that passengers can stand up and take photos. In Southern Africa, open air jeeps are used, meaning there is no roof. Having experienced both, I would say that both have their advantages and disadvantages. The open air jeep gives you a more interactive experience, a real feel of being in the bush. However, when it is really hot or cold or rainy, I'll take the jeep with a roof and A/C and heat. Also, foot safaris are not permitted in most parks in East Africa but can be achieved in many places in southern Africa.

Most first-time safari participants go to East Africa to the well-known Masai Mara and Serengeti, as well as Ngorongoro, Samburu, Amboseli, and Tsavo National Parks. They will be rewarded with lots of wildlife sightings and spectacular scenery.

While you can't go wrong on an East Africa safari, I think it is a more intimate experience in Southern Africa where there are more private game reserves. This means less tourists in any one place. The only place this is not true is in Kruger National Park, which always has lots of tourists. Private game reserves are owned or leased by private operators and range from moderate to luxurious in both amenities and pricing. There are also many other options to round out the safari experience, such as Cape Town including the Cape Peninsula and Cape Point, Johannesburg, Robben Island, Limpopo, Durban, and the Cape Winelands.

There may not be much of a decision as to where to go. Your safari destination may be determined by what you want to see.

For example, the Black Rhino can only be found in Etosha National Park (Namibia), Kruger National Park (South Africa), and Chobe National Park (Botswana). The highest concentration of elephants is in South Africa's Addo National Park and Chobe National Park (Botswana). If you want to see the rare white lion, the only place is in South Africa's Timbavati region. If you're looking for a birding safari, they are all over Africa, especially in Kenya's Kakameya Forest and Botswana's Okavango Delta. If you want to see Victoria Falls, you have to go to Zambia and Zimbabwe. If you want a gorilla safari, you will go to Uganda or Rwanda, specifically Bwindi Impenetrable National Forest or Volcanoes National Park. If you want to go off the beaten path and are looking for the best bargain, that will be Malawi. If you're looking for maximum adventure activities, that would be South Africa, which offers unique options, such as kloofing, canopy tours, and shark cage diving.

**You may notice 'Masai' is spelled two different ways: Maasai or Masai. Both ways are acceptable.
Masai Mara National Reserve**

*   *   *

Best Safari Destinations...

As mentioned, the best safari destinations for most participants are East Africa and Southern Africa.

Here's a list of the best destinations for each place:

Southern Africa=South Africa, Botswana, Namibia, Zimbabwe, Malawi and Zambia.

East Africa=Kenya, Tanzania, Uganda and Rwanda.

Here is a list of highlights of each of these places:

Botswana: As far as tourism is concerned, this country is divided into five regions (Northern, Central, Kgalagadi, Eastern, and Southern). Safari participants will mostly be interested in the Northern and Central regions.

Northern Botswana: Okavango Delta (comprised of Panhandle, Delta, and Dryland), Moremi Game Reserve, and Chobe National Park.

Central Botswana: Central Kalahari Game Reserve (one of largest in the world), Kgalagadi Transfrontier Park (black-maned lion and 170 bird species), Makgadikgadi Pans National Park, and The Kgalagadi.

Best Park in Botswana: Chobe National Park is the third largest park in the country. It is the most biologically diverse with large numbers of birds, reptiles, and mammals, including the Kalahari Elephant. This is the largest in size of all known elephant species. A wide array of safaris are offered including boat safaris, canoe safaris, and game drives (classic safaris) where the Big Five (huge elephant population but low

rhino population) can be seen.
http://www.botswanatourism.co.bw/

Kenya (East Africa): For the sake of tourism, it can be divided into Coastal Kenya, Northern Kenya, Highlands & Valleys, Forests, and Wilderness Areas.

Highlands & Valleys: Mt. Kenya, Western Highlands, Rift Valley, and Menegai Crater.

Forests: Mt. Kenya Forest, Aberdare Forest, Kakamega Forest, and Arabuko Sokoke Forest.

Wilderness Areas: Masai Mara Game Reserve (home to Masai Mara tribe), Nairobi National Park, Samburu Game Reserve, Lake Nakuru National Park (home to thousands of flamigos), Amboseli National Park (specular views of Mt. Kilimanjaro), Buffalo Springs & Shaba National Reserve, Hell's Gate National Park, and Meru National Park.

Coastal Kenya: Tsavo East National Park and Tsavo West National Park. These two parks total roughly 8,000 miles.

Best Park in Kenya: Masai Mara National Reserve offers classic safaris where the Big Five (especially big cats) can be seen and where the annual wildebeest migration, which is the largest animal migration in the world, can be witnessed. The largest population of lions can be found in this reserve.

http://www.magicalkenya.com/

Wildebeest & Zebra Annual Migration

This event is the largest animal migration in the world. We're talking about approximately 1.5 million (1.3 million wildebeest and 200,000+ zebras) migrating roughly 1,800 miles.

Where to go to see them?
The Serengeti and Masai Mara.

When?

This depends on a myriad of factors, but some believe the best time is Jan – March.

What else should I know?

They are unpredictable! They can be seen other times and places. The animals go forwards and sideways and backwards (not in a straight line or circle, as popularly believed).

Malawi ("Warm Heart of Africa"): Lake Malawi National Park (is a UNESCO World Heritage Site and includes Mumbo Island), Liwonde National Park, Chongoni Rock Art Area (UNESCO World Heritage Site), Shire River (boat safari), Nyika National Park (wild and remote), Elephant Marsh, Majete Wildlife Reserve, Mount Mulanje, Monkey Bay, Kasungu National Park, Lengwe National Park. Malawai is separated from Mozambique and Tanzania by Lake Malawi. To its northwest is Zambia, to the northeast is Tanzania, and Mozambique is to its east, west, and south. There are several small game reserves here that has leopards, lions, hippos, and elephants, as well as lots of birds and antelopes.

Best Park in Malawai: Lake Malawi National Park has all kinds of wildlife, including vervet monkeys, warthogs, elephants, hippos, crocodiles, baboons and hyrax. There are lots of beautiful tropical fish in Lake Malawi, as well as island camps. In addition to safaris, visitors can enjoy rock climbing, trekking, fishing, snorkeling, kayaking, and more.

http://www.malawitourism.com/

Namibia: Etosha National Park (one of the biggest and best parks in Africa), Skeleton Coast National Park (seal colonies, shipwrecks, huge dunes and canyons), Namib Naukluft National Park (nearly 20,000 square miles with lagoons, granite mountains, and savannahs), Mamili National Park, Damaraland, Fish River Canyon, Waterberg National Park, and Ai-Ais/Richtersveld Transfrontier Park.

Namibia is an adventure lover's paradise. Sky diving, rock climbing, quad biking, sandboarding, and more can be accomplished here.

Best Park in Namibia: Etosha National Park offers classic safaris with the Big Five (and flamingos seasonally). The park is home to several rare animals, such as black rhinos, Gemsbok, Tsessebe, and Black-faced Impalas.

http://www.namibiatourism.org/

Namibia Safari

Rwanda: Volcanoes National Park (50 miles of lush vegetation and home to the endangered mountain gorilla and golden monkeys). It is the most patrolled park in the world and the oldest park in Africa. Other significant places: Akagera National Park, Gishwati Forest, and Nyungwe Forest National Park (East Africa's only canopy walk is offered here).

An East Africa Community Visa is now offered for those interested in traveling to Kenya, Uganda, and Rwanda. It is good for ninety days. More about this special travel visa can be found on the tourism site listed below.

Best Park in Rwanda: Volcanoes National Park is home to the mountain gorilla, as well as the golden monkey, buffalo, and spotted hyena, as well as 200 species of birds.

http://www.rwandatourism.com/

FYI: Rwanda and Uganda are where you go for gorilla safaris. You need to be in good physical shape to participate as you can trek in difficult terrain for 2 – 6 hours in search of the gorillas. If you don't avoid the rainy season, this will most likely be a wet trek.

South Africa: There are almost too many options for safaris in South Africa. Seriously! So I have narrowed it down to these top destinations: Golden Gate Highlands National

Park, Karoo National Park, Kgalagadi Transfrontier Park, Knysna National Lake Area, Mapungubwe National Park, Marakele National Park, Mokala National Park, Kruger National Park, Namaqua National Park, Table Mountain National Park, Wilderness National Park, and Ai-Ais/Richtersveld Transfrontier Park.

Also worth mentioning are Grootbos Nature Reserve (100+ bird species and 500+ plant species), Sabi Sands (many private game reserves with lots of good wildlife viewing), and Kwazulu Natal (lots of small game reserves).

Best Park in South Africa: Kruger National Park is one of the biggest parks in all of Africa with more species of animals than anywhere else: 114 types of reptiles, 147 species of mammals, and 507 species of birds (and 336 types of trees). Classic safaris are offered here where all the Big Five can be seen, as well as many other species of animals.

Note: There is Kruger National Park and Greater Kruger National Park. Greater Kruger includes all the private reserves at Kruger. Greater Kruger is where walking safaris can be achieved

http://www.southafrica.net/za/en/landing/visitor-home

Tanzania (East Africa): There are many places in Tanzania so I have narrowed the list down to the top destinations: Ngorongoro Crater Park (includes Ngorongoro Crater, which is the largest intact caldera in world), Serengeti National Park, Zanzibar ("Spice Islands" and Zanzibar Archipelago), Tarangire National Park (third largest park in Tanzania), Lake Manyara National Park, Mt. Kilimanjaro ("Roof of Africa"), Selous Game Reserve (second largest reserve in Tanzania and UNESCO World Heritage Site and great place for foot, boat, and classic safaris), Ruaha National Park, Mafia Island Marine Park, Serengeti National Park, Arusha National Park (forest animals), and Mt. Meru.

    Best Park in Tanzania: Ngorongoro Crater Conservation Area is a UNESCO World Heritage Site. Its volcanic crater is one of the seven natural wonders of Africa. Walking safaris are permitted here and offer some of the best scenery and wildlife in Tanzania.

    http://www.tanzaniatouristboard.com/

Uganda ("Pearl of Africa"): Bwindi Impenetrable Forest National Park (home to roughly 300 gorillas), Kibale National Park (rain

forest, crater lakes, and grasslands), Kidepo
Valley National Park, Lake Mburo National
Park, Mgahinga National Park, Mount Elgon
National Park, Semuliki National Park,
Rwenzori National Park, Murchison Falls
National Park, and Queen Elizabeth National
Park (volcanic crater, lakes, swamps, and rivers).

Best Park in Uganda: Kidepo Valley
National Park accommodates many species
found nowhere else in Uganda, such as the
cheetah, black-backed jackals, Burchell's Zebra,
bushduiker, waterbuck, side-striped jackals,
Cape Buffalo, and Rothschild's Giraffe. It boasts
close to 500 species of birds, including many
birds of prey, such as Egyptian Vulture and
Pygmy Falcon.

http://visituganda.com/

Zambia: South Luangwa National Park, North Luangwa National Park (both have good variety of lesser seen wildlife, such as hyenas, pukus, and elands), Liuwa Plain National Park, Lochinvar National Park, Luambe National Park, Lukusuzi National Park, Kafue National Park (one of the largest in Africa), Blue Lagoon National Park, Isangano National Park, Lusenga Plain National Park, Mosi-oa-Tunva National Park, Mweru Wantipa National Park, Kasanka National Park, Lavushi Manda National Park, Nsumbu National Park, Nyika National Park, West Lunga National Park, Sioma Ngwezi National Park, and the Lower Zambezi National Park (offers many safari options, such as boat, canoe, walking, and night safaris), including Victoria Falls.

Anything you can imagine (and then some!) can be done while at Victoria Falls, such as swimming in Devils Pool (seasonally), rafting, helicopter rides, microlighting ("Flight of Angels"), hydrospeeding, bungee jumping, gorge swinging, and abseiling. It is truly an adventure lover's paradise.

Best Park in Zambia: South Luangwa National Park has large populations of elephants, Thornicroft Giraffes, hippos, crocodiles, and

buffalos. It is one of the best parks in Africa for walking safaris and one of only a few places where night walking safaris are offered.
http://www.zambiatourism.com/

Zimbabwe: Hwange National Park (biggest park in Zimbabwe and home to diverse animal population including rhinos, elephants, and giraffes), Chizarira National Park (wild and remote), Zambezi National Park, Mt. Inyangani (highest mountain in Zimbabwe), Chimanimani National Park, Kazuma Pan National Park, Matopos National Park, Nyanga National Park, Gonarezhou National Park (wild and remote), Zambezi River (and Victoria Falls, which is twice the height of Niagara Falls and nearly twice the width is in Victoria Falls National Park), Mana Pools National Park (in Zambezi Valley), Matobo Hills National Park, Matusadona National Park, and Malilangwe Wildlife Reserve (best place to see rare species, such as sable antelope).

Just like in Zambia, there are the roughly the same amount of adventure activities offered. Also, while there you may want to check out Great Zimbabwe, an ancient city and UNESCO World Heritage Site.

Best Park in Zimbabwe: Hwange

National Park is home to the Big Five, as well as many other animals not commonly seen in other places in Africa, such as the Black-faced hunting dog, leopard, white and black rhinos, and cheetahs, as well as 50 species of raptors, that can be seen during classic safaris. This park is the size of the country of Wales. It is the oldest and largest in the country. It was named after a local Nhanzwa Chief, Hwange Roseumbani.

http://www.zimbabwetourism.net/

How about adding an island stay onto your safari?

Lots of folks choose to finish their safari with a short stay on one of Africa's lovely islands. In addition to resort activities, there are national parks, reserves, and abundant wildlife on these islands. Here is a list of the best African islands:

Madagascar: This is the fourth largest island in the world with unique ecosystem and hundreds of rare or endangered wildlife (including 103 lemur species, forest elephants, giant forest hogs, two dozen species of bats, 200 species of butterflies, and 300+ species of birds) and unique flora and fauna. National Parks include: Amber Mountain, Andohahela, Zombitse-Vohibasia, Zahamena, Tsimanampetsotse, Bemaraha, Isalo, Perinet Reserve, Mantadia, Marojeijy, Ranomafana, Namoroka, Midongy du sud, Masoala, Andringitra, Ankarafantsika, Baie de Baly, and Kirindy Mitea. http://www.world-guides.com/africa/madagascar/

Mauritius: This is a bustling, luxurious island full of five-star resort hotels, specialty restaurants, and beautiful beaches. National Parks include Black River Gorges, Islets, and Bras d'Eau. http://www.mauritius.net/index.php

Mozambique: It is known for snorkeling, great scuba diving, whale watching, birding, and world-class game fishing, as well as the Bazaruto Archipelago (Bazaruto, Benguerra, and Margaruque Islands). National Parks include Gorongosa, Niassa, Banhine, Bazaruto, Limpopo, Magoe, Zinave, and Quirimbas. http://www.visitmozambique.net/

Republic of Seychelles: This is a compilation of 115 islands in the western Indian Ocean. Tourists flock to Felicite, Fregate, Cousine, Denis, Bird, Desroches, Mahe, Praslin, and La Digue. While it has become a popular destination with the rich and famous, the Seychelles has a wide range of affordable hotels, self-caterings and charming Creole guesthouses. National Parks include Baie Ternay, Curieuse, Ile Coco, Morne Seychelles, Port Launay, Praslin, Silhouette, and Ste. Anne. http://www.seychelles.travel/

Zanzibar: This Indian Ocean Island is only twenty or so miles from Tanzania. Some claim it has the best fishing, diving and snorkeling in the world. Stone Town is historical and picturesque.

There are a few small reserves, including Zala, Kiwengwa, and Ngezi, as well as seven marine parks. The only national park on the island is the Jozani Chwaka Bay National Park. This 20-mile park is home to many species of birds and monkeys, as well as flora and fauna.
http://www.zanzibartourism.net/

Mountain gorillas
(Uganda & Rwanda)

A **UNESCO World Heritage Site** is a place
(such as a forest, mountain, lake, island, desert,
monument, building, complex, or city)
that is listed by the United Nations Educational,
Scientific and Cultural Organization (UNESCO) as of
special cultural or physical significance (see list of
World Heritage Sites). There are quite a few such places
in Africa, including Okavango Delta, Victoria Falls,
Ngoronoro Conservation Area, Bwindi Impenetrable
Forest, Tsingy Reserve, Mana Pools, and Mt.
Kilimanjaro.

For a complete list:
http://en.wikipedia.org/wiki/List_of_World_Heritage_Sit
es_in_Africaa

Here is a list of different types of safaris. For
certain safaris, you will not have a choice. For
example, foot safaris are what you'll do in

Madagascar. You will trek if you choose a gorilla safari. You will participate in game drives in Kenya.

Driving safaris (also known as overland safaris): typically participants book a safari package and upon arrival they are met by their guide and driver, who takes them from reserve to reserve (or park) where they will see wildlife during **game drives**. These overland safari packages are offered by tour operators specializing in travel to Africa. This is the most popular safari option. There is a list of tour operators in the back of this reference.

    Specialty Safaris are another option. Travelers can create their own customized safari or work with a travel agent to create a special safari just for them. This can be a private safari or one that is simply independent, meaning you may be in a small group sometimes but you are not traveling with the same group throughout as you do on an overland safari. Even if you plan to book a safari package, you should be aware of all the options so that you can put together the best possible trip. For most travelers, this is a once in a lifetime trip so you want to be sure you know about every opportunity, such as an extension to Victoria Falls or a short stay at an

African island resort at the end of your safari.

Some folks think this option is more expensive, but I have put together customized safaris that cost less than most safari packages.

Self-drive safaris are for those who are comfortable traveling independently and who feel they can handle whatever might happen. In other words, you are truly on your own. You plan your own trip, book the trip, rent a car, and drive yourself wherever you plan to go.

I don't recommend this option for most folks for several reasons. For one thing, this is not the same as traveling on your own in Europe or the U.S. These are developing countries with a completely different tourism infrastructure. Some of these areas are not safe for tourists or have poor roads that can be difficult to navigate. However, if you are determined this is what you want to do, be meticulous in your planning. Stick to main roads and parks. That said, most parks are in remote places so there is always a chance you will get lost or run out of gas or get a flat tire.

Make sure you are ready in case of an emergency. Be sure to have at least one spare tire, extra fuel, food, water, and a first aid kit. Be sure you have left your itinerary with a trusted friend or family member before you depart so that if anything happens, they will have some idea of where you are.

For those with limited time and unlimited funds, **fly-in safaris** are an option. There are charter flights that take participants right to the game reserve or park. This is also a good option for visiting places that are practically inaccessible even in an all-terrain vehicle. It's also good for maximizing your time as flying is always faster than driving. These are usually offered in Namibia, Botswana, Zambia, and Zimbabwe.

Walking safaris are different from bush walks. Bush walks (South Africa, Botswana, and Namibia) are the equivalent to a game drive, which lasts 2-3 hours. Foot safaris are extended game drives whereby you might be walking through a portion of a game reserve for most of a day. In other words, your safari experience is on foot rather than in a jeep or a boat. You are walking in the wilds of Africa! You are having an authentic safari experience, like safari participants used to have once upon a time. These special safaris are only offered in Zimbabwe and Zambia.

A few places permit elephant-back safaris. Instead of achieving your safari on foot or through game drive, you do it on an elephant. **The best place for an elephant-back safari is the Okavango Delta in Botswana.**

Another option is a **canoe safari**. The best places for canoe safaris are on the Okavango River in the Okavango Delta and the Zambezi River (Zambia and Zimbabwe). Participants leisurely float down the river in mokoros with guides pointing out wildlife.

Botswana Canoe Safari

Boat safaris are offered in Malawi, Zimbabwe, Botswana, and Zambia. More about boat and cruise safaris can be found in the back of this reference.

Hot-air balloon safaris are offered many places throughout Africa, but I think the best is East Africa over the Northern Serengeti. You will watch the sun rise over the Serengeti and see so much wildlife—it is just a thrilling experience! Some places in South Africa offer them but make sure they are wildlife safaris as some of those are scenic rides over the winelands and townships. Typically, the rides last 2-3 hours and take place in the early morning. Note that you may have to miss a game drive in order to participate in the balloon safari, but it is worth it! Often, a champagne breakfast is served in the bush.

Camel safaris are another option participants can choose in Namibia, Kenya and

Tanzania. They are typically led by local tribesman and riding a camel is a memorable experience!

Or you can opt to take a **horseback safari or a biking safari,** but this is only a good option for experienced riders.

For the less adventurous, there are cruise lines that offer good African itineraries, as well as **safari cruises** on the Zambezi River or Nile River.

NOTE: Additional activities can be booked through a tour operator or your travel agent or through the lodge or on your own. These are wonderful activities that enhance your safari experience. They include a hot-air balloon flight, conversation center visit, elephant encounter, fishing at Lake Victoria, Victoria Falls cruise, helicopter ride, visits to local schools or villages, shark cage diving, bush walks (same as a game drive but go on foot rather than in a jeep), and much more (depending on the destination) can be added on to these packages. Be sure to inquire about optional activities when you book your package.

About Lodging...

Accommodations in Africa are as diverse as the topography and people. One option is a **mobile tent safari.** As the name suggests, the camp is mobile. Upon arrival at the next destination, you will find the staff has already arrived and set up camp. But there is no "roughing it" as you will have hot showers, good food, lovely tents, and bar service. Another option is **participatory camping** whereby you help set up and break down camp, as well as help prepare meals. This is a great option for budget-minded and adventurous travelers. There are not as many amenities but the trade-off is the authentic safari experience. You are camping in the bush!

Another option is that your small group will move from location to location but will stay in **lodges**, such as Kampala Lodge in South Africa or you may stay in **permanent tented camps,** such as Gorilla Sanctuary Camp in Uganda. You are accompanied by a knowledgeable guide and driver. These lodges and camps range from two-star to five-star and the price is in accordance with its rating.

Five Great Places For Family Safaris

South Africa, Kenya, and Tanzania are the best places for families. One important reason is that the road system is good. The lodges are equipped for kids with swimming pools and buffets, which will ensure that all dietary restrictions are covered, as well as satisfying even the pickiest child. Also, you are guaranteed to see the most variety of animals in their parks and reserves. Kruger National Park, which is the size of New Jersey, is a highlight. Best of all, South Africa has many malaria free game parks and no required inoculations. Medical care is excellent in East Africa and South Africa, in case of an emergency.

In addition to safari, you can enjoy the beautiful beaches at South Africa's Cape and in Mombasa (Kenya) and Zanzibar (Tanzania).

There are age restrictions on most safaris, which is typically twelve years old. However, if you book an independent package safari, you may bring children under twelve years old. I do not recommend bringing children under eight years old as they are too young to fully appreciate and enjoy and are not up to the challenges of adventure travel, such as long drives and flights.

When wildlife is spotted, the guide will stop and you are expected to keep quiet or talk softly so as not to spook the animals. Small children are hard to keep quiet when they're excited or unhappy, but you need to make every effort in fairness to other safari participants. You cannot bring children under twelve years old on a canoe safari, bush walk, foot safari, or balloon safari.

Furthermore, some lodges and camps have age minimums due to the close proximity of wildlife. So always be sure to check age minimums on lodging, game drives, and special activities.

Ways to make sure to keep your child content and engaged include giving them a camera to take photographs, bring along bottled water and snacks, give each child a checklist and award your children stickers for every animal he/she spots, and make sure they are and properly dressed (hat, coat or whatever). Pick a family-friendly lodge so that there are activities and options for kids during the rest of the time they were not be on game drives.

Here are five places that are especially family friendly and offer unique experiences:

Cape Town's V & A Waterfront with Table Mountain in the background

1. Tswalu, Northern Cape

Tswalu is remote since it is on the edge of the Kalahari Desert. Most fly into this reserve since is more than five hundred miles from Cape Town. It is South Africa's largest private game reserve, malaria-free, and super deluxe. They offer a special Junior Ranger program for kids. They receive their own backpacks with tools and other cool stuff upon arrival. Special activities include bush walks (including animal tracking), archery (including making bows and arrows), horseback riding, swimming pool, training, and cooking their own bush dinner. Even younger children are permitted on game drives here. Parents will also like their family suites and

round-the-clock babysitting services.
http://www.tswalu.com/

**There are spectacular statues and carvings, such as
this leopard, all over Sun City.**

2. Sun City, North-West Province

One of the few places that offers babysitting
services and a kids' club, Camp Kwena, so that
parents can have some time on their own.
There is a small zoo, children's game arcade,
waterpark, food court, Pilanesberg National Park
(where children over the age of five can enjoy an
elephant ride), shopping, restaurants, and more.
http://www.sun-city-south-africa.com/

3. Fugitive's Drift, Kwazulu-Natal

If you're looking for a fun and educational experience, this is the place. They offer a children's battlefield tour that includes visits to Zulu villages where kids can see spear and rifle demonstrations, bird watching, swimming pool, and game drives and bush walks.
http://www.fugitives-drift-lodge.com/

The Zulu people reside mostly in the KwaZulu-Natal Province. However, some Zulu can also be found in Zambia, Tanzania, Zimbabwe, and Mozambique.

4. **Masai Mara National Park**.
   Gamewatchers Safaris offers fun family safaris featuring special activities for kids and teens, such as their Adventurers Club for 'Under 12', which includes building a mini-Masai home, making African masks, and bush treasure hunts. Additionally, orienteering, bush walks, and other age appropriate activities are offered for 12-17- year olds.

http://www.porini.com/kenya.html?sub=kenya-family-safari

5. **Kruger National Park** has family-oriented safaris that include game drives in enclosed vehicles, babysitting services, elephant rides/safaris, swimming pool, zip lining, wall climbing, and more. http://www.krugerpark.co.za/Kruger_Park _Family_Lodge_Safari-travel/ethnic-rustic-ambience-safari.html

When you arrive, guides are waiting to whisk you off to your lodge or camp to begin your safari adventure.

For a complete list of parks throughout Africa, go to
http://en.wikipedia.org/wiki/List_of_national_parks_in_Africa

For **tourism information** for Africa, check out
http://www.africa.com/travel/

For **trip reviews and other helpful info**, visit
http://www.tripadvisor.com/Tourism-g6-Africa-Vacations.html

*   *   *

Five Rules of Safari Etiquette

1. Don't be a quitter. You probably aren't going to see all of the "Big Five" on your first game drive, so don't go into the experience with that kind of mindset. Instead, be appreciative of all you see—and the fact that you are on an African Safari! That said, if there is a specific animal you really want to see, be sure to convey that to your guide/tracker. He/she will do their best (and probably succeed) in tracking that animal for you. Be sure to remember all that your guide/tracker does at tip time. Also, remember that you are not on a private safari (unless you are) so you must respect the wishes of other safari participants as they must respect yours.

2. Don't stand up or hop out of the jeep or do anything else without the permission of your driver. Animals will charge if they feel threatened and you can't believe how fast most can move! I recall one time that we had trouble outrunning a charging mother elephant. We were sitting calmly taking photos as they crossed the road. We hadn't done anything to provoke this elephant, as far as I could tell. However,

when the last of the herd had safely retreated into the trees, she turned without warning and came charging towards us. She cleared the distance to our jeep in no time. Our driver gunned it but she was well within a few feet by the time she decided she had made her point!

3. Respect the rules of your lodge or camp. They have them for a reason.

4. Don't be a know-it-all. Just because you read a guidebook before your trip, don't think that everyone in the jeep wants to be enlightened by you. Feel share to share an occasional remark but don't get carried away. Safari is a personal experience, even when it's a group safari. The guide knows when and what to share.

5. Be mindful of electronics. Don't bring a cell phone (unless you plan to use it to take photos)! Do I really have to say that? You won't get reception and NO ONE wants to hear you talk or text. Yes, I did include a cell phone on the packing checklist but only because I know that no one will leave home without their phone. It may come in handy at the airport or for taking photos but you shouldn't fall victim

to checking emails or social media. You're on safari!

The same is true for digital cameras. Wait until you are back at the lodge or camp to go through your image library and delete unwanted photos. NO ONE wants to hear the beeping and clicking of your camera except when you're taking a photo.

Don't bring a bunch of lenses and filters unless you're on a photography safari. I am a photographer and did this on my first safari. It was a pain toting all the heavy camera gear around. The equipment is expensive so I couldn't check it or leave it anywhere and risk it getting stolen or damaged. So I had to carry it with me at all times. It was impossible to quickly add filters and change lenses. You simply don't have the time and space to properly use a 400mm or 500mm lens. Images will probably be blurry as lenses of this type need a tripod. Also, you have to shoot quickly on safari as the animals usually won't wait for you to set up your shot.

Step #2: Best Time To Go

Africa, like almost everywhere else in the world, has a rainy season. Going on safari in the rain is not that much fun, especially in certain places, such as South Africa, where you travel in open-air jeeps.

It also has a winter and summer. An important thing to remember when planning a safari is that their summer is winter for us and vice versa.

Here is a list of seasons and what to expect in each place during each season so that you can know what to expect and how to plan.

SUMMER

(December – March): is a good safari time in East Africa (Kenya and Tanzania) and in Uganda (gorilla safaris). The Great Wildebeest (and zebra and gazelle) Migration begins in December in Tanzania and Kenya. Additionally, rainfall is minimal and animals frequent watering holes during the summer months so lots of good chances to see all kinds of wildlife. There is an average of ten hours of sunshine in East Africa in February. It will be dry but hot as summer in Africa tends to be! While January and February are good gorilla safari months, March is not so avoid that time of year. However, if you plan to hike Mount Kilimanjaro, the best months are January – March and September – October. Avoid these months if going to Malawi as the rainy season is November – April.

FALL

(Late March, April and May): begins the rainy season in much of Africa, especially East Africa. However, it is also the best time to find good deals. This is also when everything is green and blooming and the babies are born. I had one of my best safari experiences in April. Our jeep did get stuck a few times on muddy roads but we didn't have much rain—and there were adorable baby animals everywhere. It was awesome! That said, it is the rainy season so you should expect rain if you go to Africa, especially East Africa, this time of year. Southern Africa is nice this time of year, especially Botswana and Namibia. The best time to go to Victoria Falls, the largest waterfall in Africa, is in March and April. It is located on the borders of Zambia and Zimbabwe, both are great safari spots, especially April – September.

WINTER

(June – September): is great safari time in Africa, including Kenya, Tanzania, South Africa, Botswana, Zambia, Zimbabwe and Namibia. This is their winter so it is the driest time of year. There is less vegetation so animals can be spotted easier. It is less crowded and not brutally hot like in the summer months.

However, it gets cold at night and early mornings. There is an average of 5.5 hours of sunshine in August in East Africa. Best months for safaris in Zimbabwe's Hwange National Park are July – October.

Best time to go whitewater rafting on Zambezi River is August – December due to low water and fast rapids! Best months for canoe safaris in Botswana's fame Okavango Delta is June – September.

The best time to go on safari to Namibia's Etosha National Park is May – September. The

best bird-watching takes place December –
March but it is hot!

Best safari time in South Africa is June –
September. There is little chance of rain and lots
of sunshine and nice weather—during the day.
In the early mornings and evenings, it turns
chilly.

The best time to go to Malawi is during
these months.

SPRING

(October – early December): There is a short
rainy season from November to early December.
However, October is an excellent month as it is
not too hot or cold or rainy and game viewing is
optimum in most places.

However, it is not good in Uganda and
Rwanda. So if you're going on a gorilla safari,
you need to avoid March-April and October-
November. During the rainy season it can be

difficult to climb to find the gorillas, not to mention a wet and unpleasant experience.

A good time to go to Zambia is September –mid-November and April – September. November is generally not a good safari time but birding is outstanding during this time in Botswana (Okavango Delta) due to breeding season from Nov – Feb. One of the best times is late December as spring gives way to summer. This is a great way to spend the holidays!

* * *

Step #3: How To Get The Best Price

Perhaps this should be the first chapter of this reference as this is always one of the biggest concerns and considerations of any trip. Safaris are not as expensive as you think, especially if you know what you're doing. Here are five ways to save lots of money and get the best price possible on any safari:

1. Everything I've read from other travel experts tells safari participants to go in the off season to save money. Since this is the rainy season, I don't like to give that advice. You can get really good deals (up to 40% off) and get lucky with decent weather. But you can also be unlucky with weather and this is no fun on safari. There are three travel seasons: low, high, and

off. As I have just mentioned, off season means worst time to go, so this is when the lowest prices are offered. High season means peak season or best time to go, so expect the highest prices during this time. Traveling in the low season can be a happy compromise. **I recommend going on safari during the low season as the rainy season will be over but high season has not yet kicked in**. See Step #2 for specific information.

2. **Avoid the most expensive places, such as Botswana, Namibia, Madagascar, Uganda, and Rwanda**. If there are animals there you really want to see, such as gorillas or lemurs, you will have to go to these places and will pay a premium price. However, using the resources and strategies included in this reference (including air consolidators and budget operators) will still save you money.

A great safari destination that is a big bargain is the **Republic of Malawi -** formerly known as Nyasaland - is a land locked country bordered by Zambia to the northwest, Tanzania to the northeast, and Mozambique to the east, west and south. The country gets its name from Maravi, which is one of the original Bantu tribes that inhabited the region. Malawi's climate is hot in the low lying southern areas and temperate in the northern highlands. Its official languages are English and Chichewa, and the capital city is Lilongwe.

The country is divided into three regions; the Northern, Central and Southern. The Northern region is mountainous, with the highest peaks reaching over 8,200 feet. It also has rugged escarpments, valleys and thickly forested slopes. The Central region is mainly a plateau, over 3,300-feet high, with fine upland scenery. The Southern is mostly low-lying except for the 6,890-foot high Zomba Plateau and isolated Mulanje Massif in the southeast.

Malawi offers a variety of landscapes, accessible forest reserves, wildlife and activities like water sports, trekking and game viewing in the most natural settings. In short, a trip to Malawi is nothing but a true African experience with a relatively minimal cost. Last year it received Lonely Planet's 'Top Ten Countries' Award.

Lilongwe is known as the Garden City. It is surrounded by colorful flowering trees that complement its modern architecture and parklands. The old town is built around the former village of Lilongwe, while the new town has modern commercial structures. Blantyre Mission, Mandela House, March 3 House, Chichiri Museum and the National Museum of Malawi are some of the places you can visit in Blantyre.

Great Rift Valley is one of the most spectacular sights in the country. Michiru Mountain Conservation, Fisherman's Rest, and the Lilongwe Nature Sanctuary are some of the various, breathtaking nature parks to visit. You can also check out Lake Malawi, which is the third largest lake in Africa. If you plan to visit any area near the countryside, you should have a guide with you at all times.

In addition to safaris, fishing, snorkeling, scuba diving, bird watching, swimming, and village visits are offered.

For a list of accommodations, activities, safaris, and more, visit http://www.malawitourism.com/

3. **Don't stay at luxury lodges and camps** ($$$$$). Instead, pick moderate lodges or camps ($$$). Or better still, try full service mobile camping. Guests enjoy walk-in dome tents, raised cots, wash basins, a flush toilet (this will be in a separate tent), hot-water bucket showers, and a dining tent (meals will be cooked over the campfire and served by the camp staff). As you can tell, this is not exactly roughing it! Or another option is participatory "overland" camping where participants load their own luggage, help set up camp, and lend a hand preparing meals. A true safari!

4. **Look at the bottom line**. What is included? Tips, meals, taxes, and extensions can add up. You may find that a more expensive safari was actually the better price once all the figures were tallied up. Also, scale back on add-ons if you're watching the bottom line. Carefully pick and choose your indulgences. For example, opt for the hot-air balloon safari and skip the visit to Sun City's crocodile sanctuary or vice versa.

5. **Sign up to be notified about specials offered by airlines and safari companies. Use budget operators** (see list provided in the back of this reference) to get best deals, as well as **iSafari**, a handy online safari planning tool. If you're working with a travel agent, be sure to let her know your budget and what you care most about seeing and doing. http://isafari.nathab.com/

The 3 "C's":
Cash, Cheques and Credit Cards.

How much money do you need during your trip? That depends on you and your trip. Some people are not comfortable carrying much cash while others find it very reassuring to have a lot of cash with them while traveling in case of an emergency. It also depends on what is included in your package. While some may prefer to charge everything, others try to use their card as little as possible.

Keep in mind while deciding how much cash to bring, that there are things not typically included, such as tipping, laundry, beverages, optional activities, souvenirs, airport visas, taxis, transfers (some lodges charge for pick up and drop off service), and some meals. All meals are usually included in safari camps and lodges but are not typically included in hotels, hostels, and other types of lodging.

How much cash you carry with you depends on your comfort level. Some folks don't like to have much cash on them. Others feel better knowing they are far from home with a wad of cash. For a two-week safari trip, I recommend taking a minimum of $500 in cash. But you should do whatever you are most comfortable doing. If your trip is largely all-inclusive you may want to take no more than $300. Or it may make you feel more assured to carry $800, especially if you prefer not to use your credit card any more than necessary. Definitely use your credit card for large purchases and save your cash for smaller purchases, such as snacks, tips, and souvenirs.

I recommend the 1/3 system, which is 1/3 cash in small bills, 1/3 credit card (2 different ones), and 1/3 travelers cheques.

Note: You need to authorize your credit card company to approve overseas transactions as most will block them now due to identity theft and fraud. The card issuer will ask you for dates and destinations to denote on your account. Even then, you may find they have blocked your card, which means they have frozen all activity on your account. That's why I recommend a second back-up credit card. Check the transaction fees and rates (and balances and rewards) before deciding which card to take. You can even opt for a pre-paid travel credit card. That way there is no risk with someone getting hold of the number of a high limit credit card. I recommend sticking to Visa® and MasterCard® as they are widely accepted, whereas Discover, Diner's Card®, and American Express® are not as much so.   It is often hard to access money while traveling, especially in Africa. ATMs are readily available in South Africa but not in most other countries with a few exceptions.

You can exchange cash at exchange bureaus at the airport or at a bank or even your hotel. Make sure you do that before you leave for a remote destination on your trip, such as Victoria Falls. While on safari, most lodges will accept local currency and you can charge any charges made at the lodge to your room. Typically, they don't take foreign currency or travelers cheques. They will, however, accept credit cards, at check out.

You can even exchange money before leaving home if you prefer to take care of it before you go. This can be accomplished at a large bank, such as Bank of America, or through a service, such as www.travelexinsurance.com.

You will be required to pay a deposit to reserve the trip. Typically, sixty days prior to departure, the rest of the balance is due. This date will be on the deposit contract you signed when you booked the trip. Make sure you circle the date the balance is due and put it on your calendar so that your trip doesn't get "released" (cancelled) by mistake. A good travel agent or tour operator will remind you, but things do happen.

What You Need To Know About Tipping

Staff at lodges and camps typically earn low wages. Tips are an important source of income for housekeepers, guides, and trackers. Your guide or the lodge manager will let you know about tipping. Also, there is usually a booklet or sheet in your room that will provide important information, including tipping policies. Furthermore, the tour operator will most likely also have suggested guidelines in your final documents package. Envelopes can be obtained at the front desk, but I suggest bringing them with you and having the money allocated beforehand. This way you don't have to worry about changing currency and not having enough cash on hand or figuring out who to tip and how much. You can always add money or take money out of the envelopes but it is best to have this sorted out beforehand.

Five Things You Need To Know About VAT

Another way to save money is by getting money back at the end of your trip. Yes! If you plan ahead, you can get cash back at the end of your trip. Here's what you need to know:

1. VAT is value added tax (14%). It is charged on most consumer goods, such as clothing (including purses and bags), artwork, jewelry, furniture, and many other kinds of souvenirs.
2. Most tourists can get VAT back at the end of their trip if they hold on to receipts. You will not be given receipts by street vendors but all shops will give them to you.
3. You get this back at the airport by going to the VAT office (in departure terminal) and showing your receipts. You may also be asked to show these items so make sure they are readily available. Also, make sure that all your receipts are organized and readily available before you get to the airport. This is a fairly easy and stress-free process if you do it right and well worth the effort given that a fourteen percent refund can add up if you've done much shopping!
4. DO THIS BEFORE YOU CHECK IN FOR YOUR FLIGHT. You need to do this as soon as you get to the airport, assuming your items will be in your

suitcase. Once you check your suitcase, you cannot show proof of purchases. Be sure to allow enough time as it can get busy during peak times.

5. The VAT office will not give you cash. They issue paperwork that you take to the airport exchange bureau. They will ask you what currency you want the refund in and you should say whatever the local currency is at your place of departure (such as KES=Kenyan Shilling or NAD=Namibia Dollar or TZS=Tanzanian Shilling or ZAR=South African Rand. Your inclination will be to say *your* local currency since you are headed home but the exchange rates and conversion fees are brutal. Instead get local currency and use it to shop for last minute souvenirs or have a good meal before your long flight. If you are flying out of Johannesburg, there are lots of great shops and places to eat. If you're flying out of Durban or Cape Town, there are still some good options.

*   *   *

Step #4: Book Your Safari

Now that you have decided where you want to go and when you want to go, it is time to book your trip. You will find a list of reputable companies at the back of this reference.

If you find a package from a company that is not listed in this book just be sure to do your research. This means reading the fine print. When is the trip? Check to make sure it is not during the wrong season. What is included? What is excluded? Is this company a member of an accredited organization, such as USTOA and ASTA? Do they have any complaints filed against them? Are there are customer reviews on the company's site or feedback on travel sites, such as Yelp and TripAdvisor? How long have they been in business? How long have they been offering this trip? I wouldn't book a trip with a company who just started offering a particular trip but if they've been running this trip for ten years, chances are they know what they're doing.

You can also put together a package yourself by booking directly with a lodge and booking your own flights and transfers. Whatever you do...

Bottom line: Make sure that you're in good hands.

*   *   *

Step #5: Find A Flight

If international airfare is included in your package, you can skip to Step #6. If you are making your own arrangements, I have included some resources at the end of this section to help you with this step.

Normally, fares to most African cities from the U.S., Canada and Europe run from $800 - $1,800, depending on the season and your route. That said, I have seen them higher and lower than this from time to time.

The best plan is to use airline miles you have judiciously socked away. It doesn't matter if your airline flies to your African destination or not. Nearly all airlines are in alliances these days, which means that you can fly on any of the airlines that are partners with your airline. Most major airlines are part of Star Alliance or One

World.

Take advantage of periodic specials where you can buy so many miles and get up to 100% more free. Pay your bills using a credit card that rewards you with airline miles (and then pay that card off using the money you were going to use to pay your bills). This is where the planning pays off.

If you don't have enough miles, then set up airfare alerts through **Bing, One Travel, BootsnAll Travel, STA Travel**, and **Cheap Tickets**. Do not wait for 'last minute specials' as there aren't any. Seats to Africa fill up without having to offer incentives.

FYI: You can schedule a stopover in Europe and make that a bonus to your safari! Traveling to Africa via Europe opens up dozens more options for fliers, such as Paris and Cairo. You can check your favorite travel sites, such as **Kayak, Bing, and Priceline**. Additionally, here are a few good resources for cheap airfares:

www.airlineconsolidator.com
www.cheapoair.com
www.airfarewatchdog.com
www.cheaptickets.com
www.onetravel.com
www.travelzoo.com

*   *   *

Step #6: Buy Travel Insurance

This should be obtained from a third-party company—not the tour operator you are using. You can purchase it from them if they are offering insurance from another company. Many tour operators offer third-party travel insurance as a courtesy for their travelers. <u>It must be purchased at the time of booking.</u> You cannot add it at a later date if you change your mind. It may seem a little pricey to you at five percent of the cost of your trip (on average) but that is a drop in the bucket compared to what you have paid for the trip—not to mention that peace of mind having travel insurance will give you.

This should be a comprehensive policy that includes trip cancellation and missed flights.

Good places to start are:

www.InsureMyTrip.com
www.AccessAmerica.com
www.TravelExinsurance.com
www.WorldNomads.com

Typical Safari Lodge

*   *   *

Step #7: Vaccinations

You should see your doctor and talk to him about the vaccinations you'll be getting if there are required vaccinations for your destination, especially if you're being treated for a chronic medical condition. However, it is highly unlikely that your doctor will have the vaccinations. Instead, you will need to go to your local county health department or travel clinic. They will verify what is required and recommended and then give you the vaccinations you need and want. A good starting place to learn about vaccinations is www.cdc.gov.

The most serious risk while traveling in parts of Africa is malaria, which is transmitted by infected mosquitoes. Wearing repellant and long pants and long-sleeved shirts is helpful but shouldn't be a substitute for malaria meds in high risk areas. Mosquito netting over the beds is provided at most safari camps. Additionally, most camps have slow-burning mosquito coils throughout the camp.

However, nothing takes the place of anti-malaria meds, which are different according to which region of the world you are going, so be sure to be specific about your destinations. If a yellow fever vaccination is required, they will also provide you with a yellow fever certificate, which you will have to show. For example, a yellow fever certificate is NOT needed to go to the Zambia side of Victoria Falls. But if you cross over into Zimbabwe, it may be required for you to enter certain countries, such as South Africa.

As far as drinking the water is concerned, I would stick with bottled water, even if the government says their tap water is okay. I do this everywhere I go, not just in Africa. This is one time that I do like to err on the side of caution!

For more information about health concerns:

Center for Disease Control (CDC)
http://wwwn.cdc.gov/travel/contentMalariaDrug
sPublic.aspx.

http://goafrica.about.com/od/healthandsafety/a/v
accinations.htm

(World Health Organization)
http://www.who.int/ith/

A Word About Safety...

While staying at African safari lodges and tented camps you are usually safe. Crime is low to non-existent in these places. It is always advisable to leave valuables, such as expensive jewelry and electronics, at home. Keep your camera and travel documents with you at all times or in a safe place. Hotels and lodges usually have safes where travelers can store valuables.

Reputable tour companies know what they're doing. As long as you listen to your guide and exercise common sense, you should be fine. There are only a few places that are not safe, such as Pretoria, Nairobi, the Congo, Somalia, the townships outside of Johannesburg, and a wee area of Zimbabwe. But even in these places, you are typically safe as long as you're with a tour group (except in Somalia and the Congo).

You should check with the U.S. State Department for the latest travel warnings as things do change in our world.
http://travel.state.gov/

Typical Safari Lodge

*　　　*　　　*

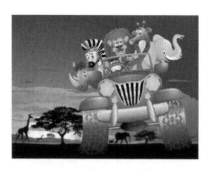

Step #8: Visas and Passports

All American traveling outside of the U.S. will need a valid passport. Typically, countries require that it be valid for six months beyond the intended length of stay. Additionally, there should be a minimum of two blank pages in your passport (check requirements for each country to ensure you have enough total blank pages).

At present, holders of American passports do not need visas for South Africa, Botswana, Rwanda, Namibia, Malawi, and Namibia.

Visas are required for Kenya, Tanzania, Uganda, Zimbabwe and Zambia. Visas for Tanzania, Zambia, and Zimbabwe may be purchased at the point of entry for a nominal fee. A Visa for Kenya can be obtained at the airport but expect a lengthy delay if you go that route. This is called an Airport Visa and is not an option for everyone but is available for U.S.

citizens. But it is better to take care of this before leaving home. You will also have to show proof of yellow fever vaccination before officials will stamp your passport and visa. For more on Visas, visit www.travisa.com and www.visacentral.com.

If your passport has expired, there has been a name change, you don't meet one of the aforementioned criteria, or you never had a passport, you will need to apply for a passport. You can imagine the bureaucratic process post-9/11. Standard processing is at least 4 – 8 weeks, but it could take longer. You can pay extra for expedited service but it is best to make sure not to leave this until the last minute as even expedited service takes approximately three weeks.

For more on passports and to obtain a downloadable application, visit http://travel.state.gov/content/passports/english/passports.html

*   *   *

Step #9: What To Pack

Packing is a challenge for many folks, especially women. We never want to get somewhere and not have the right outfit. Relax! Packing for safari is easy because it's casual—shorts, t-shirts, pants, and good walking shoes. In fact, it is recommended that you pack light.

Here is a packing checklist you can use to make this process easy:

PACKING CHECKLIST

_____t-shirts, pants, shorts, shoes
  NOTE: Clothing should be neutral or natural colors if participating in canoe safaris, bush walks, or foot safaris.
___camera/camcorder/sim card
___flashlight
___glasses/contact lenses
___book/magazines
___address labels (address labels before you leave home with mailing addresses and then put labels onto postcards; front desk at your lodge or hotel will mail for you; stamps are available in the gift shop or front desk).
___sunglasses
___hat/cap
___jacket/coat/rain slicker
___scarf & gloves
___insect repellent
___sunscreen
___hand sanitizer
___batteries
___cell phone/charger
___prescription and over the counter medications
___first aid kit
___travel documents (including passport, visas, vaccination certificate, emergency numbers, itinerary)
___money (credit cards, cash, travelers cheques)
___swimsuit and cover up
___shower/ pool shoes
___nice outfit for farewell dinner or special show/event
___safari jacket (holds everything!)
___protein bars and/or trail mix

TIP: There are travel apps to help organize and safeguard your travel documents:
https://www.tripit.com/ and
https://www.worldmate.com/

Tip: Layer up! Often it is cool in the mornings, hot during the day, and then cool again come sun down. Temperatures rise and drop fast in Africa. So, it can be cold—hot—cold within the span of one game drive. Game drives typically last two to three hours, occurring in the early a.m. and p.m.

*　　　*　　　*

Step #10: Get Psyched

The hard part is done. You have made all the important decisions, obtained all the necessary inoculations and documents, taken care of the money part—you're even packed. Now it is time to start getting excited. You are about to go on a great adventure!

So in addition to getting giddy, how about doing a little reading about where you're going? There are lots of great stories set in Africa.

The last time I was in South Africa, I discovered Author Tony Park, who writes suspense/thriller novels, all based in Africa: ***The Delta, The Prey, Far Horizon, Safari*** and his latest, ***The Hunter***. My favorite is ***Safari.*** I have to include his website because there is a great photo of him sitting at a table in the middle of

the bush writing his latest book. My dream!
http://www.southafrica.net/blog/en/posts/entry/a
uthor-tony-parks-south-africa.

I am a huge fan of Alexander McCall
Smith's series, *#1 Ladies Detective Agency*, The
books feature a lady detective and her assistant,
who share a space with a car repair garage in
Botswana. When they're not 'detecting' they
spend a lot of time drinking bush tea and
pondering why people are the way they are. I
think there are a dozen or so books in this series.

I also like the Mrs. Polifax series by
Dorothy Gilman. She is an older lady who likes
to knit and travel, as well as being a secret
government spy! Several of her books take place
in Africa, such as *Mrs. Polifax on Safari* and
Amazing Mrs. Polifax and the Lion Killer.

I have read *Out of Africa* countless times.
It is the remarkable true story of Karen Blixen's
life and her struggles to make a success of the
coffee plantation she established in the Ngong
hill country. She wrote it using the pen name,
Isak Dinesen.

Another heart-warming memoir is Kuki
Gallman's *I Dreamed Of Africa.*

What is the What is a fictional novel
about the Lost Boys of the Sudan and how they

survived a civil war and an incredible journey across Africa. There are lots of non-fiction books for kids and adults that tell the remarkable story of the Lost Boys. Just do a search through your favorite bookseller for "Lost Boys of Sudan." ***Dark Safari*** is about the story of Henry Morton's journey to Africa to find David Livingstone, who went in search of the source of the Nile River.

Two books that gave rise to the adventure genre and inspired future safari books and films was H. Rider Haggard's ***King Solomon's Mines*** (1885) and ***Five Weeks in a Balloon*** by Jules Verne (1863).

*   *   *

Safari Animals Checklist

You're going to see so many animals that you won't be able to remember them all! Guides will point out mammals, amphibians, reptiles, and birds—big and small and high and low!

Be sure to 'Print and Save' this handy checklist. Fill in the circle if you see the animal. Some of these species can only be found in select parks or reserves and this list does not include bird, snake, or most reptile species as there are simply too many to name, but I have left space at the end of the list so that you can add them to your list. You see so much that you don't even realize how much! This checklist helps you keep track of all you've seen throughout your safari.

Safari Animals Checklist

- Aardvark
- Antelope (Roan)
- Antelope (Sable)
- Baboon (Chacma)
- Baboon (Olive)
- Baboon (Yellow)
- Buffalo (African Cape)
- Bushbaby (Lesser)
- Bushbaby (Thick-tailed)
- Bushbuck
- Bushpig
- Caracal
- Cat (African Wild)
- Cat (Small spotted)
- Cheetah
- Chimpanzee
- Civet (African)
- Colobus
- Crocodile (Nile)
- Dik Dik
- Dog (Wild)
- Duiker
- Eland
- Elephant
- Fox (Bat-eared)
- Fox (Cape)
- Gazelle (Grant's)

○Gazelle (Thomson's)
○Gemsbok
○Genet
○Gerenuk
○Giraffe (Masai)
○Giraffe (Reticulated)
○Giraffe (Rothschild's)
○Giraffe (Thonicroft)
○Gorilla (Lowland)
○Gorilla (Mountain)
○Grysbok
○Hare
○Hartebeest
○Hedgehog
○Hippo
○Honey Badger
○Hyena (Brown)
○Hyena (Spotted)
○Hyena (Striped)
○Hyrax
○Impala
○Jackal (Black-backed)
○Jackal (Common)
○Jackal (Side-striped)
○Kob
○Kudu (Greater)
○Kudu (Lesser)

- Lechwe
- Leopard
- Lion
- Mongoose (Banded)
- Mongoose (Dwarf)
- Mongoose (Large Grey)
- Mongoose (Meller's)
- Mongoose (Selous)
- Mongoose (Slender)
- Mongoose (Small Grey)
- Mongoose (White-tailed)
- Mongoose (Yellow)
- Monkey (Patas)
- Monkey (Sykes)
- Monkey (Vervet)
- Nyala
- Oryx
- Ostrich
- Otter (Cape)
- Otter (Spotted)
- Pangolin
- Porcupine
- Puku
- Reedbuck (Bohor)
- Reedbuck (Common)
- Reebuck (Mountain)
- Rhebuck
- Rhino (White)

- Rhino (Black)
- Serval
- Springbok
- Squirrel (Ground)
- Squirrel (Tree)
- Steenbok
- Topi
- Warthog
- Waterbuck
- Wildebeest
- Zebra (Burchell's)

Zebra (Grevy's)
- Zebra (Mountain)

Other sightings:

-
-
-
-
-
-
-
-
-
-

**Hippos are one of the most dangerous
animals in Africa, especially when you
come across them in the water.**

*   *   *

LIST OF SAFARI COMPANIES &
SAFARI CRUISES

These companies offer trips that range from budget to deluxe and include all types of safaris and destinations. I have not included specific itineraries or prices as this information is subject to change. This is by no means a comprehensive list as there are hundreds of companies that offer trips to Africa. This is a list of companies that I am familiar with and comfortable with suggesting as good options because they are top rated tour operators with a great track record.

Abercrombie and Kent
www.abercrombiekent.com

Acacia Africa
http://www.acacia-africa.com/

Adventure Life
www.adventurelife.com

Africa Adventure Company
www.africa-adventure.com

Africa Safari
www.africasafari.com

African Travel Inc.
http://www.africantravelinc.com/

Big Five Tours & Expeditions
http://www.bigfive.com/region/africa-and-middle-east/

Bush and Beyond
http://www.bush-and-beyond.com/

Disney Adventures
www.disneyadventures.com

Djoser
http://www.djoserusa.com/

Expert Africa Inc.
www.expertafrica.com

Friendly Planet Travel
www.friendlyplanet.com

Gamewatchers Safaris
http://www.porini.com/

Gap Adventures
http://www.gadventures.com/

GeoEx (formerly Geographic Expeditions)
www.geoex.com

Go2Africa
www.Go2Africa.com

GoWay
www.goway.com

International Expeditions
www.IEtravel.com

International Wildlife Adventures
http://www.wildlifeadventures.com/

Intrepid Travel
http://www.intrepidtravel.com/us

Micato Safaris
www.micato.com

Monograms
www.monograms.com

Mountain Travel Sobek
www.mtsobek.com/

National Geographic Adventures
www.nationalgeographicadventures.com

Natural Habitats
www.nathab.com

Overseas Adventure Travel
www.oat.com

Rothschild Safaris
www.rothschildsafaris.com

Safari Now
www.safarinow.com

Thompsons Holidays
http://www.thompsons.co.za/

Tour Vacations To Go
www.tourvacationstogo.com

Wilderness Travel
www.wildernesstravel.com

Zambezi Safari & Travel Co.
www.zambezi.com

Zicasso Travel
www.zicasso.com

RESOURCES

East African Tourism: Rwanda, Burundi, Kenya, Tanzania and Uganda, www.eastafricantourism.com

South African Tourism: Botswana, Namibia, South Africa, Malawi, Zambia, and Zimbabwe, http://www.satsa.com/

*   *   *

African Cruises and Boat Safaris

You can opt for a cruise to Africa, if you prefer cruises to land travel. But you won't see much given the limited time in port. Most cruise lines offer at least one or two African cruises.

All the major cruise lines, such as Carnival and Celebrity offer similar itineraries (routes). I think the cruise line with the most (and best) options is Oceania Cruises (https://oceaniacruises.com/regions/africa/defaul t.aspx). It stops at Cape Town, Zanzibar, Namibia, Durban, Mombasa, Seychelles, and

Madagascar (depending on which route you select).

You have a few different options. You can book cruises directly through the cruise lines, look for deals through cruise brokers (such as Value World Tours & Cruises, www.rivercruises.net or Cruise Brothers, www.cruisebrothers.com), or work with a travel agent to book an African cruise.

Also, there are **Boat Safaris**, which are different from African cruises. Most cruise lines offer cruises that include some ports of call in Africa. Bear in mind that they can only stop at coastal towns, such as Senegal and Mozambique, so will not see the interior of Africa where most of the game reserves and parks are located.

Obviously, a boat safari takes place on a boat (not a ship), so it is a more intimate experience. Also, it is geared to wildlife watching. Typically, cruises are more about the journey than the destination. On boat safaris, participants will be up close with wildlife since they will be on the Chobe or Okavango or Nile or Zambezi Rivers—not in the middle of the ocean or skirting around Africa. It's a much more interactive experience.

Dhow Safaris offers week-long boat safaris through the Quirimbas Archipelago National Park aboard a twelve meter traditional Arab dhow. Participants will spend three nights at the incredible Ibo Island Lodge, which includes a roof top restaurant. While on this water safari, you might see humpback whales, sea turtles, all kinds of birds, and several species of sharks and dolphins, as well as other rare species indigenous to this area. Other activities include visiting a ghost town, local village visit, diving, snorkeling, bird watching, island hopping/exploring, and kayaking.
http://www.mozambiquedhowsafaris.com/

Another cruise choice is aboard the *Zambezi Queen,* which is a modern, beautiful river boat. For two or three days, you will go out in small boats to see wildlife (like jeep game drives only boat game rides!) Even when you're not on a "game drive" you'll still see lots of scenery and wildlife while you travel down the Chobe River. Animals come to the banks of the river often since it is their watering hole, so that you can see many different animals each day. For more information, visit www.zambeziqueen.com

Some other more adventurous options include:

Congo River Adventure offers a three week trip that includes many highlights of the Democratic Republic of the Congo. Lodging is in hotels and tented camps.
http://www.safariguides.com/african-safaris/safaris/congo-river-expedition-drc.php
Nile River Cruise offered by Nile Cruise Egypt is your chance to sail Cleopatra's route.
http://www.nilecruiseegypt.net/
Nile River Explorers offers all kinds of water options, such as family rafting trips, houseboat safaris, Nile River trips, Class V whitewater rafting trips, and much more,
http://raftafrica.com/
Senegal River Cruise describes itself as "*A unique African river cruise from the Atlantic to the fringes of the Sahara Desert.*"
http://www.fromhere2timbuktu.com/upcoming-trips-led-by-guy/senegal-river-cruise-october-to-may
Zambezi River Canoe Safari is a canoe safari on the mighty Zambezi.
http://www.zambezi.com/safari_type/canoe_safariss

* * *

Titles by Terrance Zepke

Travel Guidebooks:

The Encyclopedia of Cheap Travel: Save Up to 90% on Lodging, Flight, Tours, Cruises and More! (Lookout Publishing)

Terrance Talks Travel: A Pocket Guide to Adventure Travel (Safari Publishing)

Terrance Talks Travel: A Pocket Guide to African Safaris (Safari Publishing)

Terrance Talks Travel: A Pocket Guide to South Africa (Safari Publishing)

Spookiest Lighthouses: Discover America's Most Haunted Lighthouses (Safari Publishing)

Spookiest Battlefields (Safari Publishing)

Coastal South Carolina: Welcome to the Lowcountry (Pineapple Press)

Lighthouses of the Carolinas (Pineapple Press)

Coastal North Carolina: Its Enchanting Islands, Towns, and Communities (Pineapple Press)

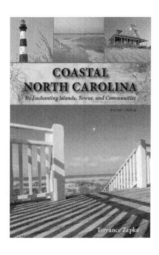

A Ghost Hunter's Guide to The Most Haunted Hotels & Inns in America (Safari Publishing)

A Ghost Hunter's Guide to The Most Haunted Houses in America (Safari Publishing)

A Ghost Hunter's Guide to The Most Haunted Places in America (Safari Publishing)

Ghost Books:

The Best Ghost Tales of South Carolina (Pineapple Press)

Ghosts of the Carolina Coasts (Pineapple Press)

Ghosts and Legends of the Carolina Coasts (Pineapple Press)

The Best Ghost Tales of North Carolina (Pineapple Press)

Ghosts of Savannah (Pineapple Press)

Special Interest Titles:

Lowcountry Voodoo: Tales, Spells and Boo Hags (Pineapple Press)

Happy Halloween! Hundreds of Perfect Party Recipes, Delightful Decorating Ideas & Awesome Activities (Safari Publishing)

Pirates of the Carolinas (Pineapple Press)

Books for Kids (8 – 12 years old)

Ghosts of the Carolinas for Kids (Pineapple Press)

Pirates of the Carolinas for Kids (Pineapple Press)

Lighthouses of the Carolinas for Kids (Pineapple Press)

*   *   *

For more information on these books and for FREE TRAVEL REPORTS:

www.terrancetalkstravel.com and www.terrancezepke.com

You can listen to her travel show at www.blogtalkradio.com/terrancealkstravel.

Follow @TerranceZepke on Twitter to receive #terrancetalkstravel tips.

You can also connect with her on Facebook. Google+ and Pinterest.

*   *   *

Safari = Journey

Safari is a Swahili word that means "to journey." It became a part of the English language in the late 1850s, thanks to a famous explorer named Richard Francis Burton.

Notes

TERRANCE ZEPKE

Notes

Notes

TERRANCE ZEPKE

Notes

Index

Safari Publishing

Made in the USA
Charleston, SC
24 May 2015